From the: Governing Grief Series

Life After Life
Heart on Fire
New Dream Journal

Anna M Hayes

Life After Life Heart on Fire New Dream Journal is a work of my own creation.

The information in this book was correct at the time of publication, and the Author does not assume any liability for loss or damage caused by errors or omissions, again, this is my perspective, opinion, and experience, so it has been written as such.

ISBN - 978-1-961185-04-3

www.inomniaparatuspublishing.com

Dedication

This Journal is dedicated to each and every person who has ever shown me a different path.

It may not have been the path I would have chosen for myself, but I learned valuable lessons along the way that I may otherwise have missed.

So, if I have not appreciated your efforts, please let me do so now.

If your efforts were to wish me harm rather than good, I pray you find a better way to your own path of healing, light and love.

I am grateful for my journey, even though I have experienced heartbreak and pain.

I am grateful for my journey because now I have learned how to love and enjoy this life after all my other lives in this world.

I am grateful for God giving me another chance to live a better and fuller life while I'm here!

Acknowledgements

To my grandparents for teaching me peace

To my parents for teaching me independence

To my sisters for teaching me how to stand up and fight

To my children for teaching me patience and determination

To my grandchildren for teaching me to let go while hanging on

To my friends for teaching me loyalty

To you for teaching me fun

And most of all; to God for teaching me to love

Your heart is on fire!
You want something more.

Who Are You and
And What Do You Want?

It's easy to say you want to make a change. It's easy to think about making changes. Yet, when it comes right down to doing it, will you really do it?

Change isn't easy, especially after any type of tragedy or traumatic experience. Often we get trapped in a "new normal" of devastation, guilt, telling ourselves "never again will I...", negativity and often self-deprecation or even harm.

Why do we do that to ourselves? Why do we continue to punish ourselves over something we most likely had no control over?

Any type of loss will be followed by grief; there's no bypassing those feelings and you need to feel them. A severe loss such as the death of a loved one can be devastating and is something you will never get over, yet you can learn to build a new dream to live comfortably in.

How do I know this? Because I did! I hear you; you may be saying to yourself that I have no idea what you've been through. No, I don't have any idea what you've been through and I may never know. My experience and yours can never be compared.

1

What I do know is that the trauma I lived through was quite devastating to me and I'm sure yours is to you as well. What I do know is that no matter what the circumstances, you have the ability to re-write your story to be one of magic and miracles just by looking at it through a different set of eyes.

There are thousands of people out there teaching the art of manifestation. Honestly, I'm sure they all have it right, at least for them.

What I want to show you is how to teach yourself to do what's best for you and how to find what works for you and you alone. We are not cookie-cutter molds of animal crackers. We have individual ways of thinking, being, reasoning, knowing and showing up.

It's well known that it takes 21 days to form a new habit, but do you know that on average it takes at least 90 days to keep that habit going and 12 months to fully form that habit in our brains?

Often times, the negative habit is so ingrained in our brains that we need constant maintenance reminders to keep that habit from ever coming back. Hence why most 12-step programs are continued each week or month for life.

Changing a negative habit can sometimes lead to an identity crisis. Yup, you read this correctly. You may experience a full-on crisis of who you are as you make the necessary changes to move on with your new chapters to your new dream life.

So when I asked you, "Who are you and what do you want?", the answer to that question is subject to change without notice.

This journal is best used with my book, "Life After Life; New Chapters, New Dream. Live It With Your Heart On Fire", but can easily be used without it.

Each section is set to be used as a monthly guide to build upon your new dream. As I stated before, it generally takes a full 12 months to fully ingrain a new habit.

Here are some suggestions for each month. Use what works for you. If you don't find something that works for you, please feel free to ask questions on my Facebook Page @ www.facebook.com/annahayes.thebeautywithin for other suggestions.

I will add that physical fitness is non-negotiable, but the others are merely suggestions. You can use whatever you like in place of those suggestions, but your physical fitness is imperative in order to make the necessary changes you will need for your new dream!

I'm not saying you have to start training for the Ironman Triathlon, just begin or increase your physical fitness journey to a new and more expansive part of your daily routine.

The first page will start you with your first steps for the month.

Set your intention for the dream you want to make in your life. Be as specific as possible. You may want to start with only one aspect of your dream such as what size you want to be, where you want to live, how much money you want to make, or what kind of romantic partner you want in your life.

Once your intention is set, write it down on your "Next Step" page.

Example:
My intention is to lose 10 pounds this month.
My first step is: to cut my portions.
My second step is: to watch my sugar intake.
My third step is: to follow a daily exercise regimen and slowly increase it.

Remember to keep track of your progress and reward yourself (preferably not with chocolate cake if you're trying to lose 10 lbs).

Keep notes on the note pages for each week of the month on how your journey is going; the good and the not-so-good.

Be sure to be kind to yourself. If you miss a day, don't beat yourself up. It took you a long time to get to where you are. Give yourself some grace to get to where you're going.

Have faith, have fun and above all else, start believing you are having the life you want with your heart on fire!

I am only one step away from my new dream!

Month 1

What's my next step?

Monthly *Planner*

Notes

······················
······················
······················
······················
······················
······················
······················
······················
······················
······················
······················

Habit Tracker

Physical Fitness ●●●●●●●●●●●

Insert new habit ●●●●●●●●●●●

Insert new habit ●●●●●●●●●●●

Write down everything you're grateful for now
at the beginning of Month 1.
You can add to this as you want.

THIS MONTH'S *Gratitude* JAR

NOTES

Date:

NOTES

Date:

NOTES

Date:

NOTES

Date:

NOTES

Date:

This is where you appreciate everything that happened
for you and to you that you are thankful for at the end of month 1!

FILL THE MONTH WITH *Gratitude*

MONTH:

ALL THE SMALL THINGS I APPRECIATED THIS? MONTH	ALL THE GOOD THINGS THAT HAPPENED THIS MONTH

THIS MONTH'S POSTIVE AFFIRMATIONS	MY FAVORITE MOMENTS OF THE MONTH

Congratulations!

You have completed your
first month of life change!

Welcome to Month Two!

Look at you go! You did it and you should be proud of every little achievement you've made toward your new dream.

Remember, this is a journey of new perspectives, new ideas and learning to live outside your box.

You get to try new things, meet new people and engage in new ideas that you might not have had a chance to do before.

This is your time to shine!

Continue to improve on what you started in Month One and now you can add something new to your dream.

Your steps may not look like much now, but they will add up. So, what's your next step? Are you going to read a good book, start attending a new club, or maybe change the style of your closet? Whatever it is, make sure you fully embrace the gratitude of and in everything you do.

I am only one step away from my new dream!

What's my next step?

Monthly *Planner*

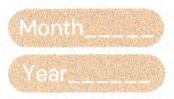

Month_____

Year_____

Notes

....
....
....
....
....
....
....
....
....
....
....

Habit Tracker

Physical Fitness

Insert new habit

Insert new habit

17

*Write down everything you're grateful for now
at the beginning of Month 2.
You can add to this as you want.*

THIS MONTH'S *Gratitude* **JAR**

NOTES

Date:

NOTES

Date:

NOTES

Date:

NOTES

NOTES

Date:

This is where you appreciate everything that happened
for you and to you that you are thankful for at the end of month 1!

FILL THE MONTH WITH *Gratitude*

MONTH:

ALL THE SMALL THINGS I APPRECIATED THIS? MONTH	ALL THE GOOD THINGS THAT HAPPENED THIS MONTH

THIS MONTH'S POSTIVE AFFIRMATIONS	MY FAVORITE MOMENTS OF THE MONTH

Congratulatons!

You have completed your second month of life change!

Welcome to Month Three!

Check you out! You've made it to Month 3. I'll bet it's been an interesting ride, hasn't it?

About this time, your brain and your body are working in unison to get you off track. You've probably thought more than a few times about tossing this journal to the side and just guiltily casting a glance at it from time to time, am I right?

Yet, you are not going to do that this time! You are determined to make the changes you want to make and nothing and no one are going to stop you.

You are going to stand on this journal like your life depends upon it because guess what? IT DOES!

You are going to climb this mountain with every breath you have in you, even if it feels like your bones are breaking and your muscles are tearing apart because the option of falling back is deadly and you're not about to cave in.

(Little dramatic? Hmmm, maybe.)

So, what's your next step?

Remember to keep up with your past steps and build upon them with each new step you take.

I'm rooting for you!

I am only one step away from my new dream!

What's my next step?

27

Monthly *Planner*

Month_____
Year_____

Notes

·····································
·····································
·····································
·····································
·····································
·····································
·····································
·····································
·····································
·····································
·····································
·····································

Habit Tracker

Physical Fitness

Insert new habit

Insert new habit

Write down everything you're grateful for now
at the beginning of Month 3.
You can add to this as you want.

THIS MONTH'S *Gratitude* **JAR**

THINGS I FEEL THANKFUL FOR

NOTES

NOTES

Date:

NOTES

NOTES

Date:

NOTES

Date:

This is where you appreciate everything that happened
for you and to you that you are thankful for at the end of Month 3!

FILL THE MONTH WITH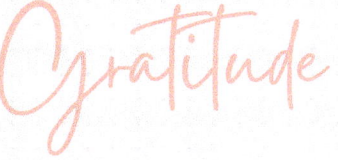

MONTH:

ALL THE SMALL THINGS I APPRECIATED THIS? MONTH	ALL THE GOOD THINGS THAT HAPPENED THIS MONTH

THIS MONTH'S POSTIVE AFFIRMATIONS	MY FAVORITE MOMENTS OF THE MONTH

Congratulatons!

You have completed your third month of life change!

Welcome to Month Four!

Whew! You made it through the first huge hurdle; that 3 month mark. You are well on your way to building some great new habits.

So, what do you need next for your new dream. What is it that will propel you to where you want to go?

Think of this month as another month one; like you're starting fresh with a new set of goals. This does not mean slacking on your last three months. You need to keep those habits up and running in a continuous cycle.

So maybe now you need to focus on some of your interpersonal relationships, or how about learning a new skill (professional or personal)?

This is a good time to go over that first question I asked you; "Who Are You And What Do You Want?"

Really think about what you've already achieved in the last three months and how you can build on those accomplishments to level up.

Now, what's your next step?

Remember, you are not alone. Join my tribe of like-minded individuals who are also making changes to level up.

I am only one step away from my new dream!

Month 4

What's my next step?

Monthly *Planner*

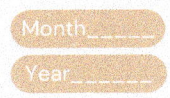
Month_____
Year_____

Notes

....
....
....
....
....
....
....
....
....
....

Habit Tracker

Physical Fitness
⬤⬤⬤⬤⬤⬤⬤⬤⬤⬤⬤
⬤⬤⬤⬤⬤⬤⬤⬤⬤⬤⬤
⬤⬤⬤⬤⬤⬤⬤⬤⬤⬤⬤

⬤⬤⬤⬤⬤⬤⬤⬤⬤⬤⬤
_____ ⬤⬤⬤⬤⬤⬤⬤⬤⬤⬤⬤
Insert new habit

⬤⬤⬤⬤⬤⬤⬤⬤⬤⬤⬤
_____ ⬤⬤⬤⬤⬤⬤⬤⬤⬤⬤⬤
Insert new habit

Write down everything you're grateful for now
at the beginning of Month 4.
You can add to this as you want.

THIS MONTH'S *Gratitude* JAR

THINGS I FEEL
THANKFUL FOR

NOTES

Date:

NOTES

Date:

NOTES

NOTES

Date:

NOTES

Date:

This is where you appreciate everything that happened
for you and to you that you are thankful for at the end of Month 4!

FILL THE MONTH WITH *Gratitude*

MONTH:

ALL THE SMALL THINGS I APPRECIATED THIS? MONTH	ALL THE GOOD THINGS THAT HAPPENED THIS MONTH

THIS MONTH'S POSTIVE AFFIRMATIONS	MY FAVORITE MOMENTS OF THE MONTH

Congratulatons!

You have completed your
fourth month of life change!

Welcome to Month Five!

You are a rockstar of unparalleled status! Yes, I really mean that. Do you know how hard you have worked?

Take a look in the mirror. Look at that bold, brazen, adventurous, amazing person looking back at you. You have conquered so much in such a short time.

I know it seems crazy that you've come so far, and I know that sometimes you feel like a complete phony, but you really have made such an incredible difference in just a few short months and I am so very excited for you to continue on this journey!

Since you did a little self reflection last month, I would like for you to take a little time this month and actually ask some of your closest people (family, friends, co-workers) what changes they've seen in you that have had a **positive** effect in you and your relationships.

This one can be a little scary, but I want you to make sure those you speak with are being completely honest with you. The last thing you want is someone sugar-coating the truth to spare your feelings.

Just remember, if people are being outright rude, it may be because they feel like you're leaving them behind with your new-found freedom life. Don't take this personally and don't let it push you backward. Maybe you can purchase this journal for them and let them know they too have the opportunity to make their lives better!

Now, what's your next step?

I am only one step away from my new dream!

Month 5

What's my next step?

49

Monthly *Planner*

Month_____
Year_____

Notes

....
....
....
....
....
....
....
....
....
....

Habit Tracker

Physical Fitness

⬤⬤⬤⬤⬤⬤⬤⬤⬤⬤⬤
⬤⬤⬤⬤⬤⬤⬤⬤⬤⬤⬤
⬤⬤⬤⬤⬤⬤⬤⬤⬤⬤⬤

_ _ _ _ _ _ _ _ _ _ _
Insert new habit

⬤⬤⬤⬤⬤⬤⬤⬤⬤⬤⬤
⬤⬤⬤⬤⬤⬤⬤⬤⬤⬤⬤
⬤⬤⬤⬤⬤⬤⬤⬤⬤⬤⬤

_ _ _ _ _ _ _ _ _ _ _
Insert new habit

⬤⬤⬤⬤⬤⬤⬤⬤⬤⬤⬤
⬤⬤⬤⬤⬤⬤⬤⬤⬤⬤⬤
⬤⬤⬤⬤⬤⬤⬤⬤⬤⬤⬤

Write down everything you're grateful for now
at the beginning of Month 5.
You can add to this as you want.

THIS MONTH'S *Gratitude* **JAR**

THINGS I FEEL THANKFUL FOR

NOTES

Date:

NOTES

Date:

NOTES

Date:

NOTES

Date:

NOTES

This is where you appreciate everything that happened
for you and to you that you are thankful for at the end of Month 5!

FILL THE MONTH WITH *Gratitude*

MONTH:

ALL THE SMALL THINGS I APPRECIATED THIS? MONTH	ALL THE GOOD THINGS THAT HAPPENED THIS MONTH

THIS MONTH'S POSTIVE AFFIRMATIONS	MY FAVORITE MOMENTS OF THE MONTH

Congratulatons!

You have completed your fifth month of life change!

Welcome to Month Six!

Oh My Goodness! You are half way there!!!!!!

So, how have the last six months been? It's time to ask the question again.

Who Are You and What Do You Want?

Remember, I said you may have a different idea of how to answer this question as you move along this journey.

Now, think very hard about your next steps. What changes do you need to really make for your dream to come true?

Here's a little checklist, just don't forget to keep up with what you've already started:

✔ Fitness
....

✔ Financial
....

✔ Interpersonal Relationships
....

✔ Forgiveness
....

✔ Skillset
....

✔ Network
....

✔ Mentorship
....

✔ Coaching
....

Figure out what you need next and get to work on your steps.

I am only one step away from my new dream!

Month 6

What's my next step?

60

Monthly Planner

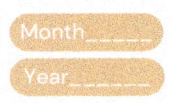

Month _____
Year _____

Notes

....
....
....
....
....
....
....
....
....
....
....
....

Habit Tracker

Physical Fitness

_____
Insert new habit

_____
Insert new habit

*Write down everything you're grateful for now
at the beginning of Month 6.
You can add to this as you want.*

THIS MONTH'S *Gratitude* JAR

NOTES

Date:

NOTES

Date:

....
....
....
....
....
....
....
....
....
....
....
....
....
....
....
....
....
....
....
....
....
....

NOTES

Date:

NOTES

Date:

NOTES

Date:

This is where you appreciate everything that happened
for you and to you that you are thankful for at the end of Month 6!

FILL THE MONTH WITH *Gratitude*

MONTH:

ALL THE SMALL THINGS I APPRECIATED THIS? MONTH

ALL THE GOOD THINGS THAT HAPPENED THIS MONTH

THIS MONTH'S POSTIVE AFFIRMATIONS

MY FAVORITE MOMENTS OF THE MONTH

Congratulatons!

You have completed your sixth month of life change!

Welcome to Month Seven!

Well, are you seeing a difference in yourself? You should be!

Take a moment and reflect on how you feel, inside and out. Go ahead and look in the mirror and check out the confidence you see building up, the happiness you can see exuding from your smile, the light you see shining from the gleam in your eyes.

Yes, that's really you!

You are becoming who you were meant to be!

All the hard times you've gone through, all the heartache, all the pain, all the fear, all the sadness; they have all stacked upon each other merely to build the mountain you are climbing now to reach new levels of joy in your life.

How can you possibly know what true happiness is unless you've experienced trauma, tragedy and trouble?

You couldn't. You would never have recognized it.

You are building an amazing new dream where you can now shift the scales of tragedy into triumph!

Your steps are getting steeper and you're able to start accessing them with ease. You have built a deeper and stronger assurance in your brain, your soul, your spirit and your body to overcome the challenges life throws at you and you have defeated them.

Does that mean you won't fall every so often? Not in the least, but it does mean you'll be able to get up easier.

I am only one step away from my new dream!

What's my next step?

Monthly *Planner*

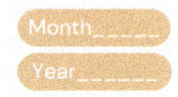

Month_____
Year_____

Notes

....
....
....
....
....
....
....
....
....
....
....

Habit Tracker

Physical Fitness ●●●●●●●●●●●●
●●●●●●●●●●●●
●●●●●●●●●●●●

●●●●●●●●●●●●
_____
Insert new habit ●●●●●●●●●●●●

●●●●●●●●●●●●
_____
Insert new habit ●●●●●●●●●●●●

Write down everything you're grateful for now
at the beginning of Month 7.
You can add to this as you want.

THIS MONTH'S *Gratitude* **JAR**

THINGS I FEEL
THANKFUL FOR

NOTES

Date:

NOTES

Date:

NOTES

Date:

NOTES

NOTES

This is where you appreciate everything that happened
for you and to you that you are thankful for at the end of Month 7!

FILL THE MONTH WITH *Gratitude*

MONTH:

ALL THE SMALL THINGS I APPRECIATED THIS? MONTH	ALL THE GOOD THINGS THAT HAPPENED THIS MONTH

THIS MONTH'S POSTIVE AFFIRMATIONS	MY FAVORITE MOMENTS OF THE MONTH

Congratulations!

You have completed your
seventh month of life change!

Welcome to Month Eight!

Your getting closer to realizing your new dream. Are you excited? I'm so excited for you!

You've had some ups and downs and I'm sure there have been people who have totally tried to stop you in your tracks, haven't they?

Yet, there have been others who have reached out a helping hand to lift you up, bring you out of the funk and show you another way.

Those are the people you need to align yourself with. The people who can see your vision with you and help you find a path that aligns with your new dream.

I'm not saying you need to dump your old, loyal friends or family. Indeed not! But for those who cannot see your vision and try to "save you from yourself" you need to set **their** fears aside and put them in a box while you position yourself with strength in the numbers of those who've paved the way before you.

Remember, you're still building your path. Get that "Caution" tape out and use it to keep the kids from stomping all over your fresh concrete.

You are the only one who gets to write your name in it!

I am only one step away from my new dream!

Month 8

What's my next step?

Monthly *Planner*

Notes

....
....
....
....
....
....
....
....
....
....
....
....
....

Habit Tracker

Physical Fitness

_____
Insert new habit

_____
Insert new habit

Write down everything you're grateful for now
at the beginning of Month 8.
You can add to this as you want.

THIS MONTH'S *Gratitude* **JAR**

THINGS I FEEL THANKFUL FOR

NOTES

Date:

NOTES

NOTES

Date:

NOTES

Date:

NOTES

This is where you appreciate everything that happened
for you and to you that you are thankful for at the end of Month 8!

FILL THE MONTH WITH *Gratitude*

MONTH:

ALL THE SMALL THINGS I APPRECIATED THIS? MONTH	ALL THE GOOD THINGS THAT HAPPENED THIS MONTH

THIS MONTH'S POSTIVE AFFIRMATIONS	MY FAVORITE MOMENTS OF THE MONTH

Congratulatons!

You have completed your
eighth month of life change!

Welcome to Month Nine!

WOW! Can you believe it? Your already rounding the 3rd quarter!

You are such a trooper and deserve a true celebration. Give yourself a high-five, a pat on the back, take yourself out to dinner or to a movie, kick back and put your feet up with a cup of whatever! You deserve to reward yourself for getting this far.

Ok, now back to stepping!

It's time to ask the question again; "Who Are You and What Do You Want?"

Think about who you've become over the last few months as opposed to who you used to be.

Go through your notes and see how your wants and needs may have changed. Has any of this changed your dream? If so, has it improved your dream or changed it into something else completely?

Now, sit down, take a deep breath and imagine with all you've learned, changed and accomplished, where do you go from here? What are your next steps to your new dream?

It's time for the big leap!

I am only one step away from my new dream!

Month 9

What's my next step?

Monthly *Planner*

Month_____

Year_____

Notes

....
....
....
....
....
....
....
....
....
....

Habit Tracker

Physical Fitness
●●●●●●●●●●
●●●●●●●●●●

Insert new habit
●●●●●●●●●●
●●●●●●●●●●

Insert new habit
●●●●●●●●●●
●●●●●●●●●●

Write down everything you're grateful for now
at the beginning of Month 9.
You can add to this as you want.

THIS MONTH'S *Gratitude* JAR

THINGS I FEEL THANKFUL FOR

NOTES

Date:

NOTES

Date:

NOTES

Date:

NOTES

Date:

NOTES

Date:

This is where you appreciate everything that happened
for you and to you that you are thankful for at the end of Month 9!

FILL THE MONTH WITH *Gratitude*

MONTH:

ALL THE SMALL THINGS I APPRECIATED THIS? MONTH	ALL THE GOOD THINGS THAT HAPPENED THIS MONTH

THIS MONTH'S POSTIVE AFFIRMATIONS	MY FAVORITE MOMENTS OF THE MONTH

Congratulatons!

You have completed your
ninth month of life change!

Big
Journeys
Begin With
Small
Steps

Welcome to Month Ten!

Last quarter and you're ready for your biggest jump into your new dream. Yes, you heard me, YOU ARE READY!

You've taken a lot of small steps. You've reflected on where you've been and where you want to go. You've looked in the mirror and seen a stem grow into a stalk ready to bear fruit or flower. You've built solid stairs up a jagged mountain.

Ask yourself now, "As I look upon all the new habits I've formed, what do they mean when I put them together?"

How can you interpret what you've built over the last nine months and how can you use it to take your next steps into your new dream?

Write down everything you've accomplished, look back at all your gratitudes, and think about what's working.

Then write down anything you think may be standing in the way of your new dream. Write down the problem or problems. For each problem, write down at least 3 solutions to that problem and then ONLY focus on the solutions.

This is where everything changes up. The next page will follow a new format for solutions.

Get to stepping, get to conquering, get to dreaming!

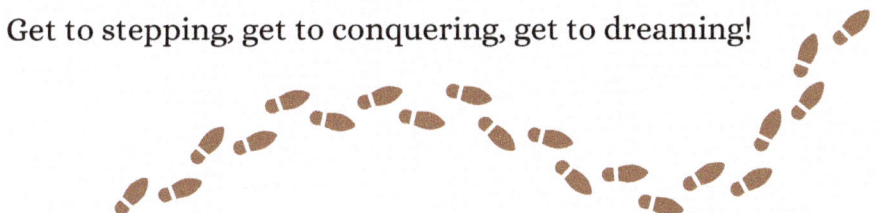

PROGRESS OVER PROBLEMS

PROBLEM(S)

SOLUTION #1	SOLUTION #2	SOLUTION #3

I am only one step away from my new dream!

What's my next step?

Monthly *Planner*

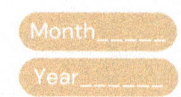

Month_____
Year_____

Notes

....
....
....
....
....
....
....
....
....
....
....
....

Habit Tracker

Physical Fitness

_____
Insert new habit

_____
Insert new habit

Write down everything you're grateful for now
at the beginning of Month 10.
You can add to this as you want.

THIS MONTH'S *Gratitude* JAR

THINGS I FEEL THANKFUL FOR

NOTES

Date:

NOTES

NOTES

NOTES

NOTES

This is where you appreciate everything that happened
for you and to you that you are thankful for at the end of Month 10!

FILL THE MONTH WITH *Gratitude*

MONTH:

ALL THE SMALL THINGS I APPRECIATED THIS? MONTH	ALL THE GOOD THINGS THAT HAPPENED THIS MONTH

THIS MONTH'S POSTIVE AFFIRMATIONS	MY FAVORITE MOMENTS OF THE MONTH

Congratulatons!

You have completed your
tenth month of life change!

PROBLEM =

SOLUTION =

Welcome to Month Eleven!

You are just burning it down with your amazing light!

You've built a strong foundation of mountain paths, learned how to shoot down incoming missiles, and now you've managed to navigate around landslides in order to keep moving forward!

You are one helluva pilot!

Does this mean life will be perfectly easy from here on out? Not by a long-shot! But you can bet your sweet peas and potatoes that you'll have an easier time understanding and accepting that what life throws at you is meant for you to live and learn and not for you to just lay down and drown.

Here's a little excerpt from my book; "Life After Life: New Chapters; New Dream. Live It With Your Heart On Fire!"

"I call my GPS 'Gypsy' because I'm often asking it 'Why, why are you taking me this way?!'

I quickly learned that the straight and narrow rarely offers grand opportunities. Sometimes you have to get lost in order to find yourself."

What are you finding as you've gotten lost in this journal and where is your new dream taking you?

What's your next step?

I am only one step away from my new dream!

Month 11

What's my next step?

Monthly *Planner*

Month_____
Year_____

Notes

....
....
....
....
....
....
....
....
....
....
....

Habit Tracker

Physical Fitness

⚪⚪⚪⚪⚪⚪⚪⚪⚪⚪⚪
⚪⚪⚪⚪⚪⚪⚪⚪⚪⚪⚪

Insert new habit

⚪⚪⚪⚪⚪⚪⚪⚪⚪⚪⚪
⚪⚪⚪⚪⚪⚪⚪⚪⚪⚪⚪

Insert new habit

⚪⚪⚪⚪⚪⚪⚪⚪⚪⚪⚪
⚪⚪⚪⚪⚪⚪⚪⚪⚪⚪⚪

Write down everything you're grateful for now
at the beginning of Month 11.
You can add to this as you want.

THIS MONTH'S *Gratitude* **JAR**

THINGS I FEEL THANKFUL FOR

NOTES

Date:

NOTES

Date:

NOTES

Date:

NOTES

NOTES

Date:

This is where you appreciate everything that happened
for you and to you that you are thankful for at the end of Month 11!

FILL THE MONTH WITH *Gratitude*

MONTH:

ALL THE SMALL THINGS I APPRECIATED THIS? MONTH	ALL THE GOOD THINGS THAT HAPPENED THIS MONTH

THIS MONTH'S POSTIVE AFFIRMATIONS	MY FAVORITE MOMENTS OF THE MONTH

Congratulations!

You have completed your eleventh month of life change!

Welcome to Month Twelve!

And now the end is near; yeah right! You're just beginning!

You, my friend, have made it to the last month of pure change in your life. Does this mean your change is over? Not a chance!

In fact, it's just beginning, again, and again, and again.

You see, what you have worked on for this year is merely a catalyst for what you keep moving forward with for not only this dream, but your next one, and then the next, and then the one after that.

There is no end to what you can dream, what you can imagine, what you can do to effect an amazing change in your life and the lives of others around you.

In this month, if you have not completed your initial dream, I urge you to continue on as long as you need to. Remember, life is a journey and the only destination is ultimately Paradise.

If you have completed one dream, then by all means, move on to the next. Get yourself another journal and keep on stepping!

Master your destiny with grace, fortitude and faith. Believe in God and believe in yourself as a child of God who's biggest commandment is to love.

Step into love this month.
Give what you've been given.

I am only one step away from my new dream!

Month 12

What's my next step?

_____
_____
_____
_____
_____
_____
_____
_____
_____
_____
_____
_____
_____
_____
_____
_____
_____
_____
_____
_____
_____

Monthly *Planner*

Month_____
Year_____

Notes

....
....
....
....
....
....
....
....
....
....
....

Habit Tracker

Physical Fitness

Insert new habit

Insert new habit

128

Write down everything you're grateful for now
at the beginning of Month 12.
You can add to this as you want.

THIS MONTH'S *Gratitude* JAR

NOTES

Date:

NOTES

Date:

NOTES

NOTES

Date:

NOTES

Date:

This is where you appreciate everything that happened
for you and to you that you are thankful for at the end of Month 12!

FILL THE MONTH WITH *Gratitude*

MONTH:

ALL THE SMALL THINGS I APPRECIATED THIS? MONTH	ALL THE GOOD THINGS THAT HAPPENED THIS MONTH

THIS MONTH'S POSTIVE AFFIRMATIONS	MY FAVORITE MOMENTS OF THE MONTH

Congratulatons!

You have completed your twelfth month of life change!

Welcome to your new dream!

Congratulations my friend. You have just made some major shifts in your life all because you made a decision to do it.

I'm sure it hasn't been easy and I'm sure you've had some doubts, but I had faith in you all along.

You may not have followed everything to a perfect "T", but you did it anyway and you should be very proud of yourself.

Sometimes it takes us awhile to really grasp the concept of change.

It can be very scary and intimidating to think that we can move out of our comfort zone and actually do something against the grain and be thankful for the pain in doing it.

I'm adding some extra note pages for your convenience. Sometimes we just need a little more and that's perfectly fine.

Always remember to dream and dream big!

Love and blessings;

NOTES

Date:

NOTES

Date:

NOTES

Date:

NOTES

NOTES

Date:

NOTES

NOTES

Date:

NOTES

NOTES

NOTES

Date:

NOTES

Date:

NOTES

NOTES

Date:

NOTES

Date:

NOTES

Date:

NOTES

NOTES

Date:

NOTES

Date:

NOTES

NOTES

Date:

NOTES

Date:

NOTES

NOTES

NOTES

Anna Hayes is a mother and grandmother living in Northern California.

She has been in funeral service for nearly 30 years caring for families during some of the worst times of their lives.

Anna is also a Certified Church Chaplain with degrees and additional certifications in Psychology, Sociology, and Early Childhood Development, Public Speaking, Celebrant Training, and Business with Employee Benefits.

She's also an author of numerous trainings and publications on grief, grieving and end-of-life planning.

Anna has also had to learn to live with loss of her own loved ones including her little sister and her father at a very young age, but the worst of all her husband and her son.

Anna's education, professional and personal experience make her uniquely qualified to help others rise above the ashes and find new life after loss.

Anna loves her life traveling and helping others to learn to move through their heartaches as she has her own.

"You'll never get over your loss, especially those you love so dearly, but you can move through and begin to live and love again"

Anna